Dedicated to Charlie

LAST NIGHT THE STRANGEST THING HAPPENED...

SOMETHING UNEXPECTEDLY!

WHEN I OPENED
THE PATIO DOORS...

WHAT DID I SEE?

A CREATURE
WAS SITTING THERE...

STARING BACK AT ME!

IT WAS THEN I HAD TO JUMP JUMP JUMP

THERE'S AN OPOSSUM!

ON THE PATIO IN THE SNOW!

I ASKED, "HEY, SHOULDN'T YOU BE SLEEPING?"

THE OPOSSUM DIDN'T ANSWER ME!

SO I ASKED MOMMY AND DADDY...

WHY THE OPOSSUM WAS VISITING ME.

MOMMY SAID HE MIGHT BE HUNGRY.

HE DIDN'T LOOK HUNGRY TO ME!

THE OPOSSUM TURNED TO GO...

SO AGAIN I HAD TO SAY "OH NO!"

THERE'S AN OPOSSUM ON THE PATIO...

IN THE SNOW!

WHICH MADE ME WONDER WHAT THE OPOSSUM WOULD EAT...

TO SURVIVE IN THE CANADIAN WINTERS...

MOMMY SAID OPOSSUMS EAT WHATEVER THEY CAN FIND...

I HOPED HE DIDN'T GET ANY SPLINTERS!

AND NOW IT'S TIME TO JUMP JUMP JUMP

PLEASE JOIN ME WHEN I SAY...

THERE ONCE WAS AN OPOSSUM ON THE PATIO...

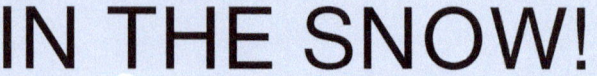

IN THE SNOW!

BUT NOW HE'S GONE AWAY!

"BYE BYE"

SEEING AN
OPOSSUM
ON THE PATIO
IN THE SNOW!

Jump Series:

Jump Like a Caribou!
Jump Like a Kangaroo!
Jump at the Zoo!
Jump and Say P.U.!
Jump and Say Boo!
Jump and Say Valentine's Day Is
For Kids Too!
Jump and Look For a Clue!
Jump and Say Happy Birthday to You!
Jump For Everything Blue!
Jump, Hop and Say Happy Easter To You!
Jump and Say Cock-A-Doodle-Do!
Jump and Sing Da-Do-Do-Do!
Jump and Ask Who? Who?
Jump and Squawk Like a Cockatoo!
Jump and Ask Is It You or Ewe?
Jump and Say There's an Ewww in My
Stew!
Jump and Say Merry Christmas To You!
Jump and Cheer Happy New Year!
Jump and Say There's a Moo-Moo in a
Tutu!
Jump and Say There's a Hare in My Hair!
Jump and Say My Aunt Ate An Ant!
Jump and Say There's An Aardvark
In The Amusement Park!
Jump and Roar For The Dinosaurs!
Jump and Buzz Like A Bee!
Jump and Flutter Like A Butterfly!
Jump and Pop Like Popcorn!

Jump and Ribbit Like A Frog!
Jump and Snore Like A Koala!
Jump and Snuffle Like A Platypus!
Jump and Grunt Like A Groundhog!
Jump and Say Hello!
Jump and Say Friend!
Jump and Say Peace!
Jump and Say Sky!
Jump and Say Merry Christmas!
Jump and Say Happy New Year!
Jump and Say Fun!
Jump and Say Family!

Clap For Series
Clap for 1!
Clap for 2!
Clap for 3!
Clap for 4!
Clap for 5!
Clap for 6!
Clap for 7!
Clap for 8!
Clap for 9!
Clap for 10!

The Cat Who Said Hello
The Three Boulders
Billy Shakespeare
Billie Shakespeare
Learn To Draw With Symmetry
ABC More Learn to Draw With Symmetry

Non-Fiction
103 Fundraising Ideas For Parent Volunteers With Schools
and Teams